Animal Welfare

What's That Got To Do With Me?

Animal Welfare

Antony Lishak

Smart Apple Media

This book has been published in cooperation
with Franklin Watts.

Series editor: Adrian Cole, Design: Thomas Keenes,
Art director: Jonathan Hair, Picture researcher: Diana Morris

Acknowledgements:
Adrian Arbib/Still Pictures: 24, 28r. Pallava
Baglia/UNEP/Still Pictures: 6l, 25. Alvaro
Barrientos/AP/Empics: 22, 23. Digital Vision: front cover tl,
back cover tr. Peter Frischmuth/Still Pictures: 9. Dennis
Galante/Corbis: 14. Dan Habib/Corbis: 12, 28l. Philippe
Hays/Rex Features: 17. Andrew Hofford/Rex Features: 2,
16. imagebroker/Alamy: 4-5. 10. LWA-JDC/Corbis: 11, 28c,
32. Dennis Marisco/Corbis: 18. Reuters/Corbis: 15, 29. Bob
Rowan/Progressive Image/Corbis: 27. William
Sallas/Duomo/Corbis: 20. Dale C Spartas/Corbis: 13, 31.
Sygma/Corbis: front cover bt, back cover br, 7, 26. Torre
Argentina Cat Sanctuary, Rome: 6c, 19. viva.org.uk: 6r, 21.
Jennie Woodward/Corbis: 8, 30.

Published in the United States by Smart Apple Media
2140 Howard Drive West, North Mankato, Minnesota 56003

Library of Congress Cataloging-in-Publication Data

Lishak, Antony.
Animal welfare / by Antony Lishak.
p. cm. — (What's that got to do with me?)
Includes index.
ISBN-13: 978-1-59920-034-7
1. Animal welfare—Juvenile literature. 2. Animal rights—
Juvenile literature. I. Title.

HV4708.L565 2007
179'.3—dc22   2006029891

9 8 7 6 5 4 3 2 1

Contents

So what?

Stories about hunting and animal experiments are never far away from the news headlines. But whether you have a pet of your own, you love to eat meat, or you feel strongly about protecting animals, issues of animal welfare remain as important as ever.

What's it all about?

Animal welfare means ensuring that people meet the needs of all animals and that animals do not experience any suffering. However, some people believe that animals should not just be protected, but that they share the same rights as people. Some animal rights supporters believe that any use of another species is wrong.

On the following pages, you will hear from a range of people with different opinions about animal welfare—from a hunter who doesn't kill mother deer because it is cruel, to a woman who works in a cat sanctuary. You will also hear from a professor who tests on animals and from an animal rights activist who doesn't believe it's right to keep pets.

Personal accounts

All of the testimonies are true. Some are first-hand accounts, while others are the result of bringing similar experiences together to create a single "voice." Wherever possible, permission to use the information has been obtained.

Ask yourself

The testimonies won't tell you all there is to know about animal welfare; that wouldn't be possible. Instead, as you encounter the different views, think about your own opinions and experiences. This will help you begin to address the question: "Animal welfare—what's that got to do with me?"

Saving a dog from a flood. People care about the welfare of animals in many ways.

An organic farm visitor

The way animals are raised and their quality of life are becoming increasingly important to people who eat meat. On a recent school visit to an organic farm, Jenny saw how some chickens are raised, and started to think a bit harder about the chicken she eats.

There were lots of chickens in the farm yard. When the farmer let us feed them, they all crowded to the fence. It felt funny to think that one of them might one day be on my plate with some peas and potatoes. But at least they were happy—well, as happy as a chicken can be. The organic farmer told

Feeding organic chickens. Organic farmers care greatly about the welfare of their birds.

Fact bank

■ Farms that rear animals naturally are called "organic." Free-range animals may still be fed with artificial food.

■ On factory farms, many birds die each year before they even reach the slaughterhouse because of poor factory conditions, crowded spaces, or cancer.

■ There are about 15 million vegetarians in the U.S., out of a total population of almost 300 million people.

Factory-farmed chickens are cheaper to raise, so the meat they produce costs less.

us that in factory farms chickens spend their whole lives crammed into overcrowded indoor pens, pecking for food on a concrete floor. Their food is mixed with chemicals and their beaks are cut off to stop them from attacking each other. Those chickens are cheaper than the ones I saw, but they do not taste as good.

My sister Jessica is a vegetarian and thinks that it's wrong to kill animals, no matter how well they are looked after. I don't agree with her. But the next time I go shopping with my mom, I'm going to read the labels on the chicken, to make sure she only buys the meat that has been well kept.

Ask yourself this . . .

■ Would you buy the more expensive, organic chicken or the cheaper, factory chicken? What factors affect your choice?

■ How important is it that animals that are killed for food are kept in good conditions?

A vet

Emily is a vet. She cares for hundreds of animals every year. As a vet, she has seen the problems caused by dog owners and breeders, who have created different pedigrees by a process of inter-breeding.

The majority of pet owners do everything they can to cater to the needs of their animals. But too many owners abuse their pets through ignorance. In my view, the worst offenders are pedigree dog owners and breeders. The unnatural process of interbreeding animals is cruel, irresponsible, and causes unnecessary suffering. I am tired of seeing Great Danes and Retrievers who are losing their sight and Dalmatians who are losing their hearing. Some

Fact bank

■ Pedigree dogs are only mated with dogs of the same breed—this can cause those dogs to have inherited weaknesses.

■ Most pedigree dogs do not develop inherited diseases.

■ Some breeders take great care only to breed healthy dogs.

Pedigree dogs are usually well cared for, but the process of interbreeding may cause problems in later life.

pedigree dogs have painful joints and breathing problems. Most Pugs and Bulldogs can't even give birth naturally because of the way their bodies have been forced to evolve over generations. Quite frankly, it's human selfishness that is causing so much distress in so many animals. We should be more concerned with the welfare of animals than the desire to have the "perfect" dog.

Many vets feel that breeding pedigree dogs is not in the best interest of the animals.

Ask yourself this . . .

■ Does it matter that the desire to breed the "perfect dog" can damage its health?

■ Should any person be allowed to keep pets?

■ Why do you think people often prefer pedigree dogs to mixed breeds?

A hunter

Jed is 12 years old and has just returned from his first whitetail-deer hunting trip with his father and his uncle. Many people around the world have the opportunity, with the correct licenses, to hunt during the hunting season.

We had to leave early, but I was so excited, I didn't sleep. Uncle George picked us up at 4 A.M.—it took an hour to get into the hills. The first thing I noticed was the quiet. It's quiet on our ranch, but you can usually hear a truck or maybe one of our dogs barking. Out there, it was silent except for the wind in the trees. That's why we had to whisper—if the deer heard anything strange, it would run. I had my own rifle with me. I'm a pretty good shot, but this felt different. It felt real. My instructions were

Hunting for the first time. For some people, hunting is part of their way of life.

Fact bank

■ In the U.S., 13% of the population hunts.

■ American hunters contribute nearly $2 million a day for wildlife conservation.

■ Many hunters have the heads of their prey stuffed and displayed as trophies.

■ Generally, hunted animals are eaten by the hunter and his family.

simple—just follow and don't speak. We spotted our first whitetail at about 8 A.M. My heart was thumping so loud I thought that maybe she would hear it! We had to make sure that she didn't have a foal with her. My dad would never kill a mother—it's too cruel. We stalked her for nearly two hours. It was Uncle George who shot her. The first bullet has to hit home or the deer just runs. Dad says that her head will be my trophy to remind me of my first hunt.

A successful hunter. Most hunters agree that the kill should be made quickly.

Ask yourself this . . .

■ Why would killing a mother deer be seen as "too cruel"?

■ Is there any difference between people who eat meat that they have killed themselves and people who buy meat from a store that has been killed for them? Why do you think that?

■ What is the difference between killing animals for food and for sport?

A professor

Professor Davison works in a laboratory that tests new medicines before they are allowed to be used on humans. This sometimes involves experimenting on animals, or "vivisection."

Not all scientists perform tests on animals.

I am an animal lover—I have two dogs that mean the world to me. Although my research sometimes involves, for example, injecting a mouse with a drug that will eventually cause its death, I would never put any animal through unnecessary distress. I am opposed to animal experimentation for cosmetics and personal care products, and I freely admit that, in the past, experiments of doubtful worth have been performed on animals that caused unacceptable pain and suffering. But I believe that

Fact bank

■ Many cosmetics companies have "not tested on animals" printed on the labels on their products.

■ Scientists are developing ways to experiment on cells taken from animals, instead of using the animals themselves.

■ In research for inherited diseases, five generations of mice can be observed in one year; in humans it would take 100 years.

■ Vaccines for measles, mumps, rubella, yellow fever, and many other illnesses were developed through animal experimentation.

my work is crucial for medical progress. It is conducted humanely, and everything I do is controlled by strict regulations. I accept that, wherever possible, animal experiments must be replaced by methods that do not use them and the number of animals in research must be reduced. But I assure you, if it meant developing a drug that would save the life of a human being, I would gladly experiment on my own dogs.

Animals, such as these monkeys, are used in some laboratory tests.

Ask yourself this . . .

■ In what circumstances, if any, is animal experimentation justified?

■ What might animal rights activist Jin Chao, featured in the following section, say to this professor about his willingness to experiment on his own dogs?

■ How do you feel when you see pictures like the one below?

An animal rights activist

Jin Chao believes that animals and humans have equal rights—and goes to extremes to protect animals from human exploitation. He feels that to campaign for animal welfare is simply not enough.

I want to end all human "exploitation" of animals. By that, I mean the raising and slaughtering of livestock, eating meat, hunting, and the use of animals for any research. I think that zoos should be shut down and dog and cat shows banned.

■ **Animal rights activists in Hong Kong.**

Fact bank

■ Animal rights activists protest outside companies that use animals.

■ Animal rights extremists go further; they attack people and property associated with animal rights abuses.

The very idea of mink being bred only so that their fur can be used in coats makes me feel sick. When I see an animal on a TV commercial or in a movie, I feel outraged. Did it ask to be used in such a way? And it doesn't matter how well any of these animals are treated—it is wrong to use a fellow creature like that. I also think the entire practice of owning pets is a complete violation of those animals' rights. If you have a dog, cat, guinea pig, or fish, they are merely prisoners in your home. And I'm not interested in animal welfare—asking for better conditions for animals that are imprisoned in farms or laboratories only encourages the murderers and experimenters. I'd much rather die of a disease than be cured by a medicine that had been tested on animals.

Protesters outside a research facility.

■ In the UK, 6,000 mink that were freed by activists devastated the local wildlife, attacking hundreds of pets and birds.

■ The Animal Liberation Front (ALF) has committed over 700 criminal acts, including vandalism, theft, and arson.

Ask yourself this . . .

■ Do you agree that all animals and humans should have equal rights? How far would you go to protect animal rights?

■ Who do you think are the "murderers and experimenters?"

■ How would your life be affected if everything Jin Chao campaigns for actually happened?

An animal shelter worker

Maria works as a volunteer at Torre Argentina, a shelter for stray and abandoned cats in Rome. Sadly, there is always a lot of work for her to do.

I have worked in the animal shelter for many years and I have seen so much cruelty. Recently, a shy cat named Stephanie left the shelter to live in front of a local store where she was fed by the kind owner. She was happy as the only cat on the street until a terrible thing happened. One man purposely let his dog approach Stephanie, causing her to hiss. The dog lunged at her and grabbed her front leg in its jaws. Everyone screamed at the man, but he was just laughing. Blood poured out of Stephanie's leg and she went into shock. A horrified lady

Cats sleeping on parked cars in Rome.

Fact bank

■ Torre Argentina cares for, sterilizes, and vaccinates approximately 2,000 cats in Rome each year.

■ Diseases can be spread to domestic cats and are mainly caused by unvaccinated populations of stray cats.

■ Organizations such as the American Society for the Prevention of Cruelty to Animals (ASPCA) campaign against cruelty to all animals. They only release animals to owners who can provide them with a safe home.

Luana and Daniele from Torre Argentina feeding cats in Rome.

rushed to the animal shelter, and three of us hurried to the scene to save the cat. Eventually, we managed to get the dog to let go. Stephanie was rushed to our vet. The man tried to run away, so I chased him. Then he tried to make his dog attack me, but it just looked up at me. We reported the man to the police. Stephanie's leg was saved, but now she is very nervous and prefers to be left alone. I doubt that we will ever find a family to adopt her. [Stephanie has since been adopted by a loving family.]

Ask yourself this . . .

■ Why do you think the work of people like Maria is so important?

■ Who is more at fault, the owner of the dog or the person who abandoned Stephanie in the first place, and why?

■ What animals would you like to help? Have you ever worked for, or contributed to, an animal shelter?

An animal lover

Gary wanted a pair of soccer cleats like David Beckham's. But Gary is also an animal lover. He found out something about the cleats, and now he is not so sure he wants them.

I sleep in a David Beckham shirt and most of the posters in my room are of him, too—the rest are of my favorite animals. I wanted to get the cleats that he wears for my birthday, but I'm not so sure now. I just found out that the shoes are from kangaroo skin. Of course, I do know that leather comes from animals, but why kangaroo skin?

The company that makes them says that "k-leather," as they call it, is the best type for soccer shoes because it is light and flexible. But Viva, the animal rights group that is campaigning against them, says that when hunters shoot female kangaroos they take any joeys out of their pouches and batter them to death. They also say that the kangaroo population is falling dramatically. Imagine Australia with no kangaroos—that would be awful! I wonder if David Beckham knows about this?

Most people play soccer in a pair of leather shoes.

Anti-kangaroo leather Protesters take their campaign outside a sports shop.

Fact bank

■ "Viva!" stands for Vegetarians' International Voice for Animals.

■ Australian law permits the killing of 5.5 million kangaroos a year.

■ Some people estimate that there are about 60 million kangaroos in Australia, but Viva! says the actual population is closer to 20 million.

Ask yourself this . . .

■ Why do you think that, for Gary, using kangaroo leather is worse than using other types?

■ What difference would it make to Gary if David Beckham was aware that his cleats were made of kangaroo leather?

■ Is wearing leather any different than eating meat? Why do you think that?

A bullring acrobat

Alberto is a *recortadore*. It's a tradition that has been in his family for many generations. He uses his acrobatic skills in the bullring to avoid the charging bull. Unlike bullfighting, the animal leaves the ring alive.

I must say that I admire the matador. It takes lots of courage to enter a bullring with such a powerful beast. And I see real beauty in the *faena*, the "dance of death," that takes place between him and the bull. It's just the end that I have a problem with.

You have to understand, bullfighting has been part of Spanish culture for over 1,000 years. These powerful bulls have been bred for centuries, so they are nothing but fighting machines. They have little in common with domestic cattle. In fact, for the first years of their lives, they are much better off than any farm animals. They are intelligent and must be respected. It is disrespectful to kill such a noble beast, and I find the sight of the crowd cheering its slow, painful death, disgusting.

I am happy when the crowd cheers at me because of my courage and skill, but also because they are paying respect to the bull that lives.

A *recortadore* narrowly avoids a charging bull.

Fact bank

■ *Recortadores* do not use swords, unlike matadors (bullfighters).

■ Sports that involve the deaths of animals are called blood sports.

■ More than 1 million people attend bullfighting in Spain every year.

■ In the UK, many people have campaigned to ban blood sports, such as fox hunting.

Ask yourself this . . .

■ How much does the fact that Alberto doesn't harm the bull make what he does right?

■ What is the difference between bullfighting and hunting?

■ Why do you think many people love and admire bullfighting and the bullfighters?

A *recortadore* makes a spectacular dive over a bull as it charges toward him.

A Chinese medicine practitioner

Mrs. Okumura has been practicing Chinese herbal medicine for 20 years. She uses traditional medicines made from plant and animal ingredients, including products made from tigers.

For more than 2,000 years, traditional Chinese herbal medicine has used natural products. It has helped cure many ailments. Mostly we use herbs and plants, but sometimes we use animals. The tiger is just one of them.

The tiger's claws are used to help sleeplessness; the teeth are good if you have a fever; the fat can be used for

A Chinese medicine practitioner holds up some products made from tiger.

Fact bank

■ A recent survey showed that 60% of Chinese people still use traditional Chinese herbal medicines.

■ In the last 20 years, the number of tigers living in the wild has dropped from 100,000 to less than 8,000—about twice that number are kept as pets in homes across the U.S.

■ Between 1980 and 1990 in Asia, about 181,500 square miles (470,000 sq km) of forest, home to the Indian tiger, were destroyed by timber loggers.

The three tiger skins here were among other skins found by customs officials in India.

arthritis; the inside of the nose can cure small insect bites; and the bone is very good for headaches and general weaknesses. We also use the eyes to treat epilepsy; the tail can be used for skin diseases; the whiskers help with toothaches; and the brain can be used to treat laziness and pimples.

Of course, modern medicine is available in China, but many people still prefer to use traditional remedies. There are people who say that the tiger could die out completely. This may be so, but I do not think that medicine is to blame. The way that humans are destroying its habitat, that is the real problem. As you can see from all the uses I have listed, we need the tiger very much.

Ask yourself this . . .

■ Why do you think Mrs. Okumura needs the tiger? Does she care about its welfare for the right reasons?

■ Why do you think so many people refuse to use "modern" medicines?

■ How much do you think it matters if tigers become extinct?

A zoo keeper

Many people believe zoos and wildlife parks play an important role in conserving endangered animals and promoting animal welfare issues. Katie works as part of the giant panda team at the San Diego Zoo in California.

I've worked here for more than 10 years and this is the third baby panda I've seen born. It's the most exciting thing ever! And it's so important— especially because there are so few of these fantastic animals left in the wild. The main reason for this is that so much of the bamboo forests in China, their natural habitat, have been destroyed by loggers. Pandas were once hunted too, but that's illegal now. I wish that one day this new baby could be

A panda cub born at the San Diego Zoo.

Fact bank

■ On average, seven pandas are born in captivity each year.

■ About 10% of the world's panda population lives in zoos.

■ More than half of the bamboo forests where pandas live have disappeared in the last 30 years.

■ Some animal rights activists do not believe that any animals should be kept in captivity.

The San Diego Zoo covers a wide area and has large animal environments.

released into its natural habitat, but the fact is that, so far, no captive-born pandas have been reintroduced into the wild successfully. But that doesn't mean the work we do is not important. Not only does the zoo give millions of people a chance to see these unique animals, but it also provides people with an opportunity to learn more about their behavior, and the more they learn, the more chance we have of successfully returning them to where they are meant to be.

Ask yourself this . . .

■ Why do you think some people believe zoos are cruel?

■ Why is it important that zoos have the highest animal welfare standards?

■ Should animals, such as pandas, be left in the wild, even with the risk of becoming extinct?

■ How important do you think Katie's work is?

What does animal welfare have to do with me?

Whether animals are an important part of your life, or whether you try your best to avoid them, it would be practically impossible to live completely independently from them. They play a huge role in many aspects of our lives, and opinions concerning their welfare and rights are held very deeply. Should the fact that many animals are intelligent mean they have the same rights as us? Should all animals be treated the same way? Does the fact that they are capable of feeling pain mean that we should always care for them as well as possible?

Your opinion counts

Some school children, who feel very deeply about animal welfare, held a discussion about the issues raised in this book. Look at their statements on the opposite page and think about whether you agree or disagree and support your decision with reasons. Look through this book again and use all of this information to form your own opinion about animal welfare.

1. "It doesn't matter how animals are treated on farms if they are going to end up dead anyway!" Grace.

2. "Locking any pet in a cage is cruel. It's like making them a prisoner." Harry.

3. "Humans have hunted animals since the cave people—so why should we stop now?" Sanjay.

4. "I don't really care how many animals are tested on if a cure can be found for diseases such as cancer. " Nicola.

5. "Cats, rats, elephants, humans—they should all have exactly the same rights." Christopher.

6. "People who mistreat animals should have the same thing done to them." Talia.

7. "Who cares what clothes are made of—as long as they feel and look good!" Gideon.

8. "Any sport that uses animals in any way is wrong and should be banned." Jessica.

9. "Humans share the planet with millions of other creatures and we must do everything we can to care for them and protect them from harm." Aaron.

10. "I enjoy eating meat, but it doesn't mean that I don't care about animals." Harry.

Web sites

www.aspca.org
Web site of the American Society for the Prevention of Cruelty to Animals with care advice and links to programs throughout the U.S.

www.sandiegozoo.org
Find out more about the different animals at the San Diego Zoo through pictures, videos, and conservation articles.

www.animalsaustralia.org
Australia-based Web site of the Australian and New Zealand Federation of Animal Societies (ANZFAS), featuring extensive campaign news.

www.worldwildlife.org/ trade/tcm.cfm
Traditional Chinese herbal medicine page on the World Wildlife Fund (WWF) Web site, including details of WWF's endangered animal monitoring and education program.

www.romancats.com/
Web site of the Torre Argentina animal shelter in Rome, featuring news and stories about life and work at the animal shelter.

www.animalconcerns.org
A discussion-based Web site from Animal Concerns with links to different animal welfare topics, including hunting, factory farming, and laboratory animals.

Glossary

www.attra.org/
organic.html
Web site of the National Sustainable Agriculture Information Service that contains numerous articles about organic farming.

Every effort has been made to ensure that these Web sites contain no inappropriate or offensive material. However, because of the nature of the Internet, it is impossible to guarantee that the contents of these sites will not be altered. We strongly advise that Internet access be supervised by a responsible adult.

Conservation – protecting and caring for plants and animals through different activities, including captive breeding and preventing habitat destruction.

Endangered – when a group of animals is at risk of extinction.

Exploitation – when something is used or mistreated for a purpose. Animal rights activists fight against the exploitation of animals.

Extinct – when an animal species has died out completely.

Extremist – someone who will go to any lengths to achieve a goal, including criminal activity. In the past, animal extremists have set fire to buildings and attacked people with links to animal testing and factory farms.

Humane – treating an animal with care and respect.

Inherited – when something, such as a medical problem, is passed through a family line from the mother or father.

Organic – a method of farming that uses only natural ways to produce food. Organic farmers do not use artificial chemicals.

Pedigree – a record of an animal's history, showing its family tree. Pedigree animals are specially bred over a long period of time.

Rights – certain freedoms, or things, you are allowed to do. Some people believe animals should have the same rights as humans.

Sterilize – when an animal is "altered" so that it cannot produce offspring. For example, this is used to help control cat populations in many areas.

Vaccine – a special drug given to animals and humans to protect them from some diseases.

Vivisection – carrying out experiments on live animals, usually in a laboratory, as part of scientific research.

Welfare – the general consideration for the health and well-being of all living creatures.

Index